NASTY WOMAN

Samantha Nagel

The following work contains themes of mental health, eating disorders, and sexual abuse.

The National Suicide Prevention Lifeline is a national network of local crisis centers that provides free and confidential emotional support to people in suicidal crisis or emotional distress 24 hours a day, 7 days a week. We're committed to improving crisis services and advancing suicide prevention by empowering individuals, advancing professional best practices, and building awareness.
Call or text 988.

RAINN is the nation's largest anti-sexual violence organization. RAINN created and operatesthe National Sexual Assault Hotline in partnership with more than 1,000 local sexual assault service providers across the country.
Chat online at online.rainn.org or call 1-800-656-4673.

Contact the National Domestic Violence Hotline by calling 800-799-7233 or text START to 88788.

To all the people who have held me and seen me in my messy, imperfect, unsure life. I love you.

RESENTMENT

I need you
But I don't know if I want you.
You need me
And I know I need you to want me.

There's a secret compartment in my heart,
One where water overflows and
Salt stings the wounds.
I cry in secret.

Every word is cataloged,
My body like a library of memories.
The tears, the voices, the hands on my body,
Captured in my spirit.

Have you ever picked at a scab
And it never healed?
You picked,
You peeled,
You bleed more than you had to.
You never even let it scar.

I was taught to want fear over rage,
That anger was a bad word.
The fires I set,
Only to put out with my hands
Before anyone noticed
Have burned off my fingerprints.

The sight of the flames makes my heart race,
The idea of love makes me vomit.

I am raw,
I am naked,
And I would do anything for a blanket.

Years of harboring pain
Has taught me that I am special,
That I am better.
I am above
The need for love,
I am above
The need for connection.

My brain exists in a different dimension than my heart does.
I don't remember
What it feels like
To hear my heart beat.

The fire I have been deprived of
Consumes me.
I live in a chasm of heat,
I exist in a sanctuary of warmth.

To forgive
Is to excuse,
To accept
Is to stop fighting.

My hate has given me a home.
My space has given me abundance.
My resistance makes me whole.

No one ever told me
That the walls don't just keep you in,

They also keep others out.
I haven't been touched in months,
I am cold in my bones.

When the flames escape me,
When the fear leaves me,
I know that I am empty.
An abandoned home that no one cares for.

COURT ROOM

Sometimes
Women also do not realize that they have
Equal power to objectify another woman.
Sometimes
Victims do not think they can become
The prosecutor, just because they too have experienced.
It is not only men
That attack women,
Aggression does not have a gender.

ODE TO MY THIGHS

You greedy bastards.
You grow and grow, not caring about the space you take up, the material that you stretch out of place.
One time, you broke my favorite dress, a thundering shred echoed as the seams burst, the only sound remaining was my hot embarrassment through my closet walls, a silent call to be accepted and forgiven as my partner lay dreaming in the bed behind the walls.
I used to have the way you changed my body, changed my identity.
You made me wider, larger,
And everyone knows a woman shouldn't take up this much space.
O sweaty dimpled skin. I streaked chafing flesh.
You are strong! You carried me up a mountain side, around the pool on a summer day.
Your plumpness makes lovers blush, makes my figure deliciously curved and enchanting, like the apple that Eve bit in to.
I am sorry that I never saw you for what you are:
A beautiful pear that skirts flow over and tights cling to.
A mass of muscles to climb with.
A foundation to support myself with.

BLACK & WHITE

This is not the best thing that's happened to me
This is not the worst thing that's happened to me.
This is good
This is bad
This is.
Black and white thinking
Has no purpose in my joy.

Wondering when this will end,
Trying to predict what will happen
In a week
In a month
In 10 years,
Has no purpose in my serenity.
I'm making the best out of this,
Because I'm a warrior.
But
If I chose to sink into pain,
Sink into sorrow,
Sink into old habits,
That's okay too.
I have both the shovel
And the ladder.
Any hole that I dig
Any trench I fall down,
I have the tools to climb higher.
I have the equipment to
Raise above where I started.
Things might be worse in
A week,
A month,
Ten years.
Things might be better in
A week,
A month,
Ten years.
All I know
Is
That in a week,
A month,
Or ten years from now,

I will have grown my toolbox,
Gotten my equipment their own room in my house,
That's how many I will have at my disposal.

DROUGHT

So what if rain never collected.
Today, I am going to lick my dry lips and pretend that is enough
for me.
My hands are chapped from giving.
I wish I could describe true love as a whirlwind.
Instead, she has wings, but is less beautiful than a butterfly.

LONELY

Maybe it's not love,
But an inconsolable loneliness that I am not able
To fill on my own.
Maybe it's not desire,
But an aching fire pit of pain that I do not know
How to put out.
Maybe it's not even wanted,
But maybe it's that I think I need you.

IGNORED

Alone on the floor,
Clinging to the words they threw,
I wondered
If they forgot about me

GHOSTS

I talked about you in therapy again yesterday and
I hated the lump in my throat that rose when
I had to speak your name,
Your name tastes bitter on my tongue,
Your name feels metallic.
When my lips mumble your name, I might as well be bringing my
lips to yours,
Breathing down your throat, feeling your lungs expand under
me,
Begging your memory to resurrect, inviting your unkind words
to
Blanket me in the warmth of self-loathing,
Or is it more like a casket?
When the tears come as I talk about you,
About your rough hands,
About the knife by my face,
I wonder what you are doing,
How you are feeling,
If you've ever hurt another woman after me.

UNTRUE LESSONS

Within the blossom of womanhood
Is when I learned what it meant to be a woman,
Taken at the age of fifteen.
Hollow, Still, Reduced:
This is what I learned about being a woman.
The sleeping bag in the back of a Volkswagen Transporter
Scratching my back,
The weight of a man pinning me down,
The open knife next to my face,
The breeze against the trees outside,
The wet, numb feeling of tears on my face:
This is what I learned about being a woman.
The feeling as fear settles into nothing,
Struggle running as wild as the "no" that echoes in the air,
Turning to passive acceptance:
That is what I learned about being a woman.
Purple and yellow bruises against young white skin,
Feverishly hidden with guilt and shame;
Hearing my own words,
But having my mouth held closed by a man;
Arms immobilized at my side,
Legs spread wide and forced down:
This is what I learned about being a woman.
ARE YOU THERE, GOD?

Have you ever closed your eyes so tight that your face hurt?
Clasped your shaky, sweating palms together in the front of your
chest,
Felt your fingertips cutting into the backs of your hands?
Have you ever felt the carpet scrape on your knees
As you knelt at the foot of the bed

Asking God to make you better.
Do you know how it feels to cry while asking someone you can't
see to take it away?
Crouching in on yourself as you sit in a public restroom,
Silent but panicked tears running down your cheeks,
Because someone yelled something at you from their car,
And suddenly, you are being raped again.
Clutching your arms in a half-hearted hug
As you tell God to make you stop crying,
At least until you get home.
Have you ever cursed God for making your life miserable,
For making you hate your body,
Hate your life,
Hate life,
Hate God?
Have you ever cursed God and then sobbed as you asked for
forgiveness,
Eyes looking up at the ceiling,
Saying you did not mean it,
To please make you better?
Have you ever fallen asleep
While asking God to let you make it through the night,
But woken up to the sound of yourself crying,
Because you had a dream about It happening again?
Have you ever laughed while listening to someone say
That everything happens for a reason,
That God has a plan and everything that happens,
Happens for a reason,
And later closed your eyes and asked God what the reason for
this was?

RECOVERY

A carnation crumbled on the floor,
A once full house stripped of furniture,
A backyard that the dog has dug one too many times.
The forest after a fire,
Once lush and flourishing,
Now reduced to ash and skeletons.
That is how it feels to be raped.
A slick spoon carving the insides of a fresh kiwi,
Pulling a freshly planted flower,
Only to step on the petals,
And watch the roots slowly shrivel.
That must be how it feels to rape.
Empty looks,
Dissonant shrugs,
Uncomfortable laughter,
Frustrated sighs in the bedroom,
That is how it feels to live with rape.
The feeling of your own fingernails distressing your skin;
Crying while undressing;
Prayers that sound like a death plea;
Flinching when touched for too long,
Waking up to your own shaking hand flipping the light on,
Gasping for breath and terrified,
Because your dreams mirror your past.
That is what it feels like to recover from what you did.

QUIET

In the cabin she whispers
What have you done to us,
What have you done to me?
This is the place where flowers came to die,
The walls so haunted, so sick,
Not even the bees dared to enter.
I am sick
She tells me, her gray cheeks wet with
Sweat?
Tears?
I'm dying, she says, why did you leave me here?
I want to hold her, I want to comfort her,
But the same thing that always stops me
Grips my heart, digging in its talons, its fist turning red from my
streaming blood
You don't deserve to love her.
She doesn't deserve your comfort, it whispers in my ear,
Its tongue flicking speckles of spit on my neck, burning my flesh
with its hate.

That is how my inner child learned not to cry.

IRIS

Love should feel like
A flower that is in bloom,
So why do I feel like
A wilted stem with no sun?
I grew up watching others
Struggle with power,
Vowing to never do the same.
I wanted to grow up
And be a daisy,
White petals and green leaves.
Instead, when I am with him,
I am an iris;
I am purple, blue,
Bruised.

WATCHING THE CLOCK

I wish I could go back to the days that we were blind to time,
Rising with the sun,
Sleeping with the stars,
Not afraid of the dark.

WHAT IF

Maybe trauma isn't the end of the story, it's the beginning of a new story told by a new person. Or maybe my life has been broken into two parts, before and after.

I have been the sinner and the saint. The abuser and the abused. I was kicked down, and then my own phantom foot kicked me again.

I am crawling towards the sun. I am freezing and all I want is to be warm. To thaw. To feel.

Speed bumps don't stop us from enjoying the drive or the view, but it does slow us down

not a race

Sometimes I convince myself that I *was* actually raped.

Sometimes I realize I was raped repeatedly.

Sometimes I convince myself that I am better.

Am I capital H healed or am I just healed

Or maybe I'm just broken.

POWER

Why do you pretend like this?
Why do you pretend that
You are okay with who you are now?
Masking a hurt heart with a mean one.
Why do you pretend that
Your joy is a curse
And that your anger is a blessing?
Your empathy doesn't make you a doormat,
Your compassion doesn't make you stupid.
You have been taught that feelings
Are the operation of a woman,
That being too sensitive
Is an insult.
You stopped relying on your feelings,
Stopped trusting your intuition.
Your intuition was the blessing,
Your emotions were your strength,
But you let them tell you that you were cursed.
Your power is within you,
Flashing,
Yelling,
Jumping,
Waiting for you to come back to her.
You have not given away your power,
For it is not something that can be owned by anyone else,
It is not a gift of yourself that you can give,
It is not something you can donate
Or throw away.
Others may have asked you to be quiet,
To cave,
To conform,

To be less sensitive,
But it was you that decided to hush.
It was you that silenced your power,
Diminished your voice.
It was you that looked in a mirror
And decide to hate yourself.
It was you that told yourself you weren't worthy,
You that thought badly of yourself.
It was you that listened to the nastiness from the other,
You that believed it was true,
And you that ignored the love people offered for you.
Just as it was you that stripped you of your power,
It will be you to regain it.
You will be the one showering yourself with love,
You will hug yourself in the bath,
You will forgive the mistakes you made,
You will validate your thoughts,
You will honor your feelings,
You will trust your intuitions.
You will own your power.
You will accept yourself.
You will love yourself.

THE RABBIT

One time she let her ex-lover
Withdraw from alcohol on her bed
While she tried to restore him
Both contained by
The walls of her studio apartment.
She laid on her thrift store couch at night,
Her back aching from the angle,
Not feeling like she deserved to sleep.
She refused to see me,
Because she knew I'd see the dark circles underneath her eyes,
Black and blue echos
Of the love she used to have for herself,
Now given away to the man who left her.
She wore his pain like a swimsuit.
She went to work in the morning,
Using her lunch break to bring him back soup,
Desperate for him to feel nourished.
I think the soup contained bits of her soul,
Floating like carrots around the rim of the bowl.
When she looked in the mirror,
She didn't see the tired girl the world saw,
I think she saw a hero,
Her cape like a patchwork quilt
Made of the faces of those she tried to save.

COVID-19

This is not my first time being quarantined
I have lived in a house
Where the walls were a prison
The doors would open,
Only to be shut again

I remember looking through the windows
Looking at those outside
The only difference is
Now everyone else is inside too

I used to be quarantined in my body
Cursed to stay in the crime scene
Covered in my own skin
A prisoner in a hated suit

I remember my body shaking
As suppressed sobs like waves
Crashed against the shore of my body

The only difference now is
I no longer feel the need
To hide the emotions I have

I used to be quarantined in my mind
Stuck inside
With only the race of my thoughts
To keep me company

I remember my skull shaking
My brain having to work too hard

To process the words
I couldn't get out
The only difference now
Is that I can paint a room
With the colors of my words

I used to be quarantined in the dark
My eyes had adjusted
To a room with no light
But I still felt scared
Of the shadows that moved

I remember
The only difference now is
The comfort I take in night
Knowing the sun will come out again

SEVEN

I can count on my hands how many years it's been since my rape.
One.
Two.
Three.
Four.
Five.
Six.
This year it will be
Seven.
Once I heard that every seven years,
The body is made up of new cells,
The body is an entirely new body.
Does that mean this year,
I will have a body that was never touched by my rapist?
Does that mean that this year,
I get to wear new skin?
This year my organs don't reek of rape.
It's like getting a whole new wardrobe,
One that you never asked for,
But it feels like a gift when you open your closet.
When this year's anniversary comes,
I will caress my arms with my new fingerprints,
I will kiss my knees with my rejuvenated lips.
Welcome, I will whisper to my reflection,
Welcome to the Earth, my beautiful new body.

When it comes,
I don't feel happy.
How do I describe disappointment?
It isn't the body I was raped in,
It's bigger,

It's soft,
It's ugly.
How do I describe disgust?
My body now wears a name tag that my doctor comments on,
That my friends avoid commenting on.
My body now wears a name tag that says
I have gained fifty pounds.
I used to look in the mirror and see a kicked puppy,
An abused stray.
I used to look in the mirror and see skin and bones
With long blonde hair.
I used to see a girl in the mirror,
One that was sexy in the way that all young girls are:
Sinful.
Now I see the round cheeks of a woman,
The curve of a midsection,
The bloom of strong thighs.
How do I describe fat?

My new cells are not what I imagined,
It took me months to rewrite my name tag.
I have gained fifty pounds
Has now turned in to
I have lost abusive relationships,
I have lost fear and shame,
I have lost the indentation in my hands that
My keys leave when I clutch them like a dagger in the shadows of
the parking lot.
I have gained fifty pounds
Has now turned in to
I have gained back pleasure in my taste buds,
I have gained beautiful relationships,
I have gained a smile that reaches the iris of my eyes

Instead of barely showing my teeth.

My name tag no longer reads a victim,
And it no longer reads a defender either.
To be quite honest with you,
I don't know what it reads.
The last time I saw my name tag, I threw it in a fire pit
And watched it burn,
The flames reminded me to embrace my new cells.
How do I describe self-acceptance?

THE LION

Her roar was louder than her soft, gentle voice ever was.
It hurt my eardrums,
It made me want to cover my ears with my hands,
But I didn't.
She used to be timid,
She used to be prey.
No longer would she ever be preyed on,
No longer could anyone quiet her.
In her newfound boldness,
Her love was as ferocious as it was before.
Because it had never been a weakness.
Her hot, fiery breath was warm, comforting,
Impossible to ignore.
She once was a rabbit,
Sitting quietly in the grass,
Hiding, trying not move,
Trying not to breathe,
Praying she wouldn't be seen.
Her mane was wild,
The curls bouncing,
The tangles unapologetically large,
Matted with dirt and sweat.
She stood in the sun,
Stretching instead of running,
No longer afraid to take up space.
She turned to me and said,
"Never again will I be a rabbit."

THE BRUISES YOU LEFT HER
After Your Son Has a Beautiful Voice by Sierra Demulder

Once, with a hushed voice into a cell phone, she told me how you
were sick.
How she loved you and how you took care of her. How she really
believed she needed you.
How she feared losing you, and how you feared losing her. How
your love was tender, that you were the best friend she was
never looking for.
How you proposed, telling me the truth this time, that it wasn't
so much a proposal as a death threat. How you stole her diary
and yelled at her, calling her a whore, then cried and begged for
forgiveness. How you started by kicking her, always in the
stomach, never on the face. How sometimes this happened when
I was sleeping in the next room. How, when her friends praised
your gentleness, your kindness, your sweetness, she was
wondering if we knew what she did.
How, when she left, you broke into her house and choked her
and told her that you loved her. How she wanted to file a police
report, but the officer on the scene advised her not to. How self-
defense laws apply to three white men in the Bible belt, but not
to a woman who fights back. How she tried to get a restraining
order and your lawyer tried to use her stolen diaries as proof
that she was a slut.
How she had to hide in the back room of her store, telling her
coworkers to say she was not there, as you showed up
everywhere you thought she might be. How, when she called the
cops when you would park outside her house all night, they said
that you legally had not done anything wrong.
How she had to move across the country to escape you, but that
she never stopped looking over her shoulder and checking her

rearview mirror for your car with you in the driver's seat,
following her.
How the nightmares never stopped.
How the shame was the only thing that kept her warm at night.
How she prays for you in church.
The bruises you left her never changed her faith in God,
They never changed her love for her friends,
They never changed her fire for her future.
The bruises you left scarred her,
But they didn't accomplish what you wanted.

SCARS

The romance we had to keep secret
Because you still wanted your options open,
The bed you let me sleep in,
Never inviting me over
Any earlier than 10pm.
I never minded that you hogged the blankets.
Sleeping next to your body was enough,
The heat from your skin, like the dying warmth of summer,
My skin damp from sweat,
My vagina sore from meaningless sex.
Well. You said it was meaningless for you.
I would leave the sound of my phone on,
Just in case you texted me at midnight,
Asking me to come over.
I always said yes.
I feel like an empty house when I'm with you,
The door hinges open,
Inviting anyway to come inside,
To love it,
To clean the floors and hang art work.
The best you've ever given me Is to pretend to be the carpenter
that pisses on the flowers in the back of the yard,
Thinking I can't see you. I don't say anything.
When you come, it's like
The wail of a child.
You wouldn't know what happens when I come,
Because you never offered to finish what you started.
To you, it was finished.
When we fuck,
You've never been sober,
I would have remembered.

I'm not sure if I've ever been sober.
You'd think I would have remembered.
You're high out of your skull,
Your pelvis shaking like battery operated suicide.
Disassociation washes over me
Like a familiar lullaby.
I only remember when it starts
And when it's over.
When you kiss me,
When I let you kiss me,
It's like you're laying brick after dusty brick,
Adding on a second bedroom
To my already empty house.
You look at my nipples like binoculars,
You see right through them.
Your love feels like running water,
I want to catch it
But I never will.
Your tongue in my mouth
Feels like barbed wire
And I don't mind the cuts.
I wore pink underwear for you,
The kind with lace,
The kind I think you'll like.
You don't notice.

TO MY 16-YEAR-OLD SELF

I am writing to you to say that it will get better,
But things won't be perfect.
You'll sit and sob when you think back to the boy who hurt you,
a boy who seemed like a man,
But now seems like a child,
Wearing his father's shoes,
His small feet swallowed by the bigness.
It will seem oddly comical,
And strangely heartbreaking
To remember the authority in which
He was able to hurt you so deeply.
You will eventually be with someone better,
Someone that loves you for you,
Not just how you serve them.
You won't live at your parent's home forever,
Someday you will live on your own,
It will be both freeing and lonely.
You will still cry so much.
I hope that a letter will come back to me soon,
A letter from my older self,
Much like this one,
From me to you.
Maybe that is all that hope is,
You trust me to take care of the memory of me,
I trust that my future self will take care of me,
Because all of myself is in this together.
You worry about if you will fit in at school -
No, you never will,
And someday you will realize that is okay,
That being liked is not the most important thing,
Especially by those

Who you don't even value.
Someday in the future,
You will unfriend them from your Facebook,
Removing the option for validation
From the people who don't matter to you.
Yes, you like women,
And that is okay.
Yes, you like men,
And that is okay, too.
Someday you will find that
Being bisexual
Is not unheard of,
Is not being "selfish,"
Is not asking for attention.
Your sexuality is a part of your identity,
And it doesn't give you a new identity,
Because you are the same person you always were.
You will make so many mistakes.
You'll sleep with the wrong men,
You'll fall in love with women
Who will never love you back.
You'll accept the unacceptable,
Then resent yourself for it later.
Things will get better,
And they will also get worse.
It is important for me to tell you -
Your value is not contingent
On your beauty,
Or your body.
Your body is not something at an auction,
Available to the highest bidder.
Your body is not a vessel
For someone else's pleasure.

My hope for you is that
When you do your makeup in the morning,
When you put on your clothes,
When you walk down the street,
You do it for you.
My hope for me is that
I can eventually reclaim our body,
Reclaim ownership
From the men who
Think they own real estate
In our hearts and
On our flesh.

Perhaps I shouldn't say
That it gets better.
It doesn't.
It gets confusing.
It gets messy.
It gets painful,
But it certainly doesn't get worse.

Perhaps I should say,
It doesn't get better,
But you will grow.
You will grow from this pain,
And you will grow stronger.
You will grow from this loneliness,
And find yourself better connected.

To My 16-Year-Old Self,
I will never stop
Being here for you,
Just like my 30-year-old self

Will always be there for me
In the future.
We are not alone,
Because we will always
Have us.

PRAYER

Today,
I prayed with the water around my knees,
My sweat dripping down my face.
I asked
God
The Universe
The Creator
A Higher Power,
The Divine Mother,
Earth,
What to do.
Today,
I asked
It
Him
She
They
How to love without breaking.
I got no answer.
There is no answer,
Not to that question.
To love
Is to
Break.
More likely,
To love
Is to be
Risky.
Love hurts
And also
Love saves.

Love is pain
And also
Love is medicine.
I asked again,
How do I love without
Becoming one with
The one I love?
I saw the flame of my candles dance.
I heard a voice,
A voice like mine
And also
A voice like
God
The Universe
The Creator
A Higher Power,
The Divine Mother,
Earth.
The voice that was like mine
But also wasn't
Told me that I would never be alone,
That I could never be abandoned.
Because, I asked, I have you?
No,
It
Him
She
They
Said.
Because you have you.
It was true.
Who else carried my weary body
When it felt like I could continue no longer?

Me.
Who else wiped my tears
Night after night of crying?
Me.
"It's always been you."
I heard.
But then,
What about you,
Whatever the fuck you're called?
I'm sorry,
I whispered.
But then again,
I know that if you're up there,
No,
If you're here,
If you love me this much,
You don't care if I use an
English curse word.
I am greeted
With a feeling of love.
You will take care of yourself,
She told me.
And I will be there to
Comfort
And to
Guide you,
He said.
Don't worry about
The others,
The others that you love so much,
That you want to
Take care of,
It assured me.

All you have to do
Is to greet them with love
And then your worries over to me,
They instructed.

And this
This is how I learned the difference
Between
Love
And
Codependency

RED GODDESS

I bleed red,

And no, I won't hide that,
Won't lie about that,
Won't be embarrassed about that.

When I bleed red,
When it swirls in clear bath water and bubbles,
Like pomegranate magic
Around my legs, my pelvic bowl,
When it runs down my wet leg and swirls into my shower drain,
Like crimson serpents
Casting the spell of life,
When it flows from inside my womb
Like the river of strength
And beginnings and power that it is,

I think of my ancestors,
Back to the respected and revered,
Bleeding in red tents of self-love and bliss,
And also back to the shamed bodies that hid,
All because of the men who lied,
Saying that God said she was unclean, impure,
Or that blood will kill crops,
(when in reality, it is divine fertilizer)

Because I am the earth,
And so is my mother,
And her mother,
And her mother before that.
I am the creator,

The goddess who knows that the body was made in love's image,
Who knows that everything from
My beating heart
To my red blood
Is sacred,
Holy,
Divine,
Beautiful.

I bleed red
Proudly,
Lovingly,
Loudly,
In honor of all of those who bleed before me,
Some with great shame,
And some with great pride,
And all with great beauty.

MY BODY IS A HOME

The fact that my body could ever be a home to another soul came both as a relief and as a fear.

The idea that my body, my body with whom I've had such a fraught relationship with for all these years, could be someone else's safe space, haunts me and delights me.

Over the years, my body has felt

Like a traitor

    a liar

        a burden

            a mistake

        a crime scene

    Too big

Too small.

But suddenly I realized
That my body, the one that has never even felt like mine to begin with,
Could grow another human,
Could create a heartbeat, fingers and toes.
Could create a body that housed a spirit, could nurture and nourish and grow and develop.
If this is true,

If my body can do all this,

Then I can do all this.

If I can do all this for another,
Doesn't this mean I can do it for
This body?
This spirit?

SOVEREIGN BODY

There is no room for a woman in pleasure,
For a woman forced to carry a heartbeat
That she never wanted in the first place
Means that she will lose the beat of her own heart.

And isn't that the goal?
The goal for the man who sits in a palace of law - of power - of
artificial creation?
Doesn't the man who searches for control seek to quiet the
woman who embodies the force of the Earth, our ultimate
mother,
The Mother who is forced to sustain more life than she can
stand.
The Mother, who has bled dry of oil, of harvest, of rain and snow,
of fire and shelter?

Women are Mother Earth incarnate, and doesn't it make sense
that we are expected to bleed dry,
For our wombs to become unwilling homes for all to inhibit,
Our bodies resources up for the taking?

There is no room for a woman in pleasure,
For what pleasure can give birth to is more than a child of a man,
It can give birth to sexuality just for the sake of sex,
Art just for the sake of joy,
Laughter just for the sake of release,
Nurturing just for the sake of pleasure,
Spirituality in worship of the Self, not in service to a higher man.

This,
This is why a woman with pleasure is to be feared,

The joyful sound of an ecstatic woman's heartbeat to be ran
from,
The idea of a creatrix to be in control of her creation, unheard of.
What power could a woman wield if we let her be in control of
her own body,
If we let her commune with our Grand Mother?

Imagine our Grand Mother's sorrow as she observes this
monstrosity,
For woman did not come from the rib of man - man came from
the belly of a woman.
Our Grand Mother has watched the men enslave, impregnate,
force life out of, beat, control and dominate Her daughters; Just
as these men abuse the Grand Mother, they abuse Her daughters.

These men,
These men who are "pro-life" good men, honorable men, going to
heaven someday men,
Will soon realize they have hell to pay,
For our Grand Mother seems all giving, the Giving Tree content
to always being reduced to a stump, forgiving how she has been
tortured.
These men,
These men will soon see that their las pesadillas se hacen
realidad, their nightmares made real, will haunt them in the
gusting wind,
Will swallow them under a wave at angry sea,
Will poison them with the oil they steal,
Their money they crave will engulf them in flames,
Much like Her daughters
When they burned them at the stake.

You can't stop the forest fire,

You can't stop the ancestral rage rooted fold in every generation,
the vessels of unpaid Karma coming around the corner.

Perhaps,
The reproductive rights we truly seek are the rights to
reproduce the great awakening
Where the Womb, the Mothers, the Birthers, the Creators, the
Mystics, and the Healers, the Genderless Feminine
Rises,
Rises up to reclaim the power taken from them,
Giving power back to our Grand Mother.

Why is a fragile man so fearful of a woman's power?
Because
He knows that the only power he truly holds was taken from the
womb of a woman
And he knows
It is only a matter of time before she comes
To take it back.

So yes,
Maybe there will be room for women in please soon enough
after all.

The Earth, Grand Mother's vision, is it purge, to release to
destroy
What has
Purged, released, burned, destroyed her,
Then to restore,
Restore the Mystics and Healers, the Mothers and Fathers, the
Born and the Living, free from identity in a new, peaceful world,
Restore the balance of divinity of masculine and feminine,
The true meaning of law and order.

The Wild Woman, both a hunter and a gatherer, who both gives
and receives, who both creates and destroys,
Lives in all of us.

VOW

As I lay bleeding,
I make a vow
To never love
The one with the knife again.
I make a promise to never love a man
More than I love myself.
I saw a prayer,
That I will never accept love
From someone that makes me cry.
I will never be
stonewalled,
ignored,
beaten,
Or taken again.
I will not accept
lies,
cheating,
manipulation.
I will no longer accept
Abuse that has been masked as love.
This,
This is my battle cry.

ACCEPTANCE

You don't have to be loved
By those who do not
Occupy a space in your heart.
You do not need to be accepted,
To accept the truest parts of yourself.
You are free
To love yourself,
Your true self,
Not just the mask
You hang for the audience.
You have existed in a circus,
With smokes and mirrors,
Always hiding your true self,
Always reflecting what you think
The crowd wants to see.
It is time to hold your own mirror,
To face your own reflection.
What I hope to see someday
Is a woman
Who loves herself,
Every opinion,
Every scar,
Every crooked tooth
And swollen blemish.
I hope to see a woman,
A woman who is loved.
A woman who is loved,
Not by the praise
She seeks from her critics,
Not by from the cheers
She wants from her spectators.

I hope to see a woman
Who is loved
From her chapped lipped smile,
To her dainty hands,
From her tiny toes,
To her thick thighs,
From her gentle voice,
To her savage tears.
I hope to see a woman,
Authentic,
At peace,
Loved.

LETTERS TO A SURVIVOR

This poem
Isn't so much of a poem
As it is a letter,
A letter to the young person,
Much like myself,
Whose voice was taken from me,
Whose choice was taken from me,
Whose memories were taken from me,
Whose body was taken from me.

This is for you,
My beautiful and beloved
Survivor,
(And also for me)
Laying in bed,
Heart pounding,
Forehead sweating,
Lightbulb eyes swirling in the sockets,
Wondering when if you'll ever
Stop waking up like this.

This is for you,
My angel butterfly
Survivor,
(And also for the 15 year old I was and never got to be)
Crying shameful tears
Under the hot shower head until it runs cold,
Feeling like you're both trapped in this body,
And so far away from it
At the same time,
Wondering if your body will ever feel

Like yours again.

I want to tell you
That it gets better -
And then worse
And then fine
And then better
And then even better
And then somehow even worse,
And then better again.

I know you wonder if it gets better,
But what is "better," anyway?
Does better mean that
You are never phased by this thing that happened to you?
That you have forgiven and forgotten like so many people
suggest you do?
That you never cry again?
That you never get scared again?
Because no,
If that's better,
Then it doesn't get better.

But it does get beautiful.
It does get easier.
It does get less isolated.
It does get more joyous.
The moments of love and pleasure
Begin to outnumber the ones of pain and fear.
The moments of connection and bliss
Begin to grow stronger than the ones of suffering and panic.

If I could tell myself anything,

I would tell her,
You're doing the best you can,
There is nothing wrong with you,
This may feel insurmountably challenging,
But it won't be like this forever.
You will reunite with your body
In a way that's more
Sweet
More
Charming
More
Loving
More
True
That you have ever felt before.

And to my darling friend reading,
I want to tell you
That I love you,
I love your
Bravery,
Your strength,
Your tears,
Your fear,
Your sleepless nights and your nightmares,
Your broken and confused heart.
I love you,
And it may never get
"Better,"
And maybe that's because
You were never broken to begin with.

GIFT

You gave me your troubles
Like they were a homemade gift,
Wrapped in a bow,
Your eager eyes watching
To see what I thought.
You gave me your worries
Like they were a framed photograph,
You were proud of the photo
That you had taken yourself,
The photo of intangible memories
Of a person that wasn't even me.
You thought I would put it above the fireplace,
Eager to show it off.

LOVE LANGUAGE

Your body is my love language
I know how to speak in its curves
It's dips it's crevices
I know how to touch it to make your tears stop falling,
How to hold your hand and feel your pulse slow underneath my fingers.
Your body is what I listen to
When I can't sleep at night,
Restless with the sounds of my brain,
Thinking,
    Thinking,
        Thinking,
The ocean waves of your breath like a whisper,
The warmth of your chest that fills our sheets and makes my skin hot,
The vibration of your thigh against mine.
Your body is the language of mine,
Teaching me when to gasp,
When to be still,
When to surrender.
Your body is my love language,
A poet that creates stanzas in coded lines,
Messages that feel like telepathy
Letting me know you're still here.
Your body is my book, my novel, written by my favorite author
I keep my reading lamp on at night, pouring over chapter after chapter,
Not wanting to put it down,
Your skin the beautiful pages,
Your mouth the printed words,
A story I hope never ends.

UNREQUITED

a field of wildflowers
moving in the breeze,
but she'll always be my favorite sunflower.
her reaching spirit has helped me
bloom with open content.
she taught me to water my own roots
with my tears,
to feel the honest forgiveness
of the earth.
she makes music out of wind,
she makes the unnoticed sun
shine brighter.
her smile makes her stem grow longer,
every day, her petals reach farther.
she gives
without needing to take.
she moves
without leaving,
and she loves
without hating.

LETTERS FROM THE CLOSET OF A MIDDLE SCHOOL GIRL

How many times can my twelve-year-old fingers
Type the words
What if I'm gay?
Into Google
And then frantically delete it?
My fingertips know the keyboard's path, dashing from upper right
To the middle of my phone
To the left
To the middle
Isn't it funny how only the A is on the left?
How many times do I stare my hands,
And wonder what it would be like
If my hand was held by a girl instead
When I see two women together on the street,
When I see someone post something about coming out,
I don't feel happy for them;
I'm scared.
Scared because what if that won't be me?
Scared because what if that will be me?

ROSE

I can still feel her black curls in my fingers,
Can see the way she looked at me
From the corner of her eyes,
Because I was looking at her, too.
I can still feel her hand brush against my arms,
Can feel the electricity shock my skin,
And I wondered,
Is this what I have been missing all these years of pretending?

LOVE IS

The way the bird signs a song of
Joyful whispers
And
flutters its wings
In my throat.

Both the kindness
Of a schoolteacher
Helping their student
Pronounce a difficult word,
And
The echos
Of two partners
Exchanging hurried kisses,
And
It is more than this,
And
It may never look
Like this.

It is the intangible
Warmth
Of honey
And
Whiskey,
Or
The unexplained knowingness of
Two strangers,
Meeting.

It is

Electricity
That dances
In the air,
The threads of
Familiarity weaving us
Tighter
With an invisible
Thread.

It is the little girl
Looking
Up
At her father over the mound of mint
Chocolate chip ice cream
To see him
Smiling back at her.

It is the compassionate nods
At brunch
As you describe
Your recent
H e a r t b r e a k.

It is the way your heart b r e a k s.

It is the way your heart s w e l l s.

The warm bath you dip
Your body
In
To.

The sweater you

Wrap your
Shoulders
In.

The pull of falling asleep
On the couch
And waking up with the lights off
And a blanket
Over you.

The teeth you show when you smile,
The crows that
Dance
On your temples.

A dog-eared book.
A lucky jersey worn on game day.

The absence
Of fear,
The feeling of
Safety,
The embodiment of
Home.

This is what
Love
Is
To me.

WE WERE ALL EVE ONCE

You are not the first to hear it,
That voice in your head - insidious as a snake,
Willing Eve to taste the fruit
    (even though we all know this is a story,
    Taught to domesticate
    Evil,
        Bold,
            Strong women)
You listen to it daily,
Inviting the voice to dinner with you,
Hearing it say
"You know they all hate you."
You tuck it in to bed next to you,
Letting it whisper in your ear
"You know you aren't good enough,"
Causing your dreams to turn to nightmares.
           :::
Who taught you to listen to this voice?
Was it your mother, the one who commented
When you gained even a few pounds?
The one who forced you to dye your brown hair blonde, making
you sit still in the bathroom,
The bleach stinging your scalp
Because you need to be beautiful in order to be loved?

Was it your boyfriend, the one who insisted
You wear your eyeliner and mascara
Because he needed you to be beautiful in order to love you?
The one that said you didn't need to have sex with him, but
would
Ignore you,

Manipulate you,
Abuse you,
Until you eventually stripped off not just your clothes, but your identity too?

:::

Sweetheart, this voice has been stuck to your ear for too long.
Let go of the fact that you cheated on the boy who raped you.
Let go of the fact that you said the wrong thing at that party once.
Embrace the women that Eve really was,

Curious,

Loud,

Independent,

Hungry.

It's okay to be hungry for that apple, my darling.
You have been starving yourself for much too long.

Run! Run to the river, run to the trees, run all those blocks to your best friend's house, or maybe just *run* and never come back!
Exorcise that voice and keep running,
Knowing that you will never hear it again

THE COYOTE
After "The Day Lady Died" by Frank O'Hara

I sit across from the coyote in a field where the red bridge is the
only thing between us and I sob and I wonder, and I know that
this will be the moment I will always look back on for what is a
coyote if not a catalyst and what is a catalyst if not for the way
your heart feels when you can remember the before and the
after splitting your memory with a sweet soft line, the kind of
line that you sink your teeth into, or maybe it's not a line maybe
it's a rio grande, a big river that swallows you whole that you
aren't afraid to bleed into the kind of river where you enter as a
rabbit and emerge as a lion, and maybe it's the moment where I
look in the mirror and see myself instead of everyone else.

THIS LIFE

Dear little boys, wherever you are, whoever your parents are,
you were born to be yourself,
To play with dolls
Or monster trucks,
To dress in a skirt
Or a suit,
To love a man
Or a woman.

Little girls, you were born to be a reflection
Of your desires, whether that's to be a loud,
Nasty woman, or a sensitive
Quiet observer. You can become a mother,
Stay single,
Or both.

For the spirit has no gender, only true
And untrue. This life has been waiting
For you, this life is your stage and you
Designed the set.

My love, this life is your prayer. You are both talking
To the heavens and listening on
The other end. This life is an amen,
A blessed be, a namaste. This life is a promise to let you
Feel, to let you experience, to let you *be*, but
Never a promise to protect you.
This life is waiting for you to sing
Like you do in the shower, to dream like you did when you were
a child.

Do you remember how you would dream before
You learned you ~~couldn't~~ shouldn't? When you dreamt
Of going to space, or being president, of writing those books,
Of being *you*?
Who taught you to stop dreaming, to stop imagining a life you
wanted?

When did you first learn that being bold was unacceptable?
Unlovable?

Today, I give you permission to laugh again.
I want to hear your ideas, your stories, your hopes, your fears.
Today,
I give you permission to be you again.

WILD & FREE

If I could go back to visit her
I would go back to the day when
Her laughter was filled with joy
Instead of masked discomfort.
I would long to visit the days of being her true self,
Playing pretend alone in the arroyos,
Visiting fairy world and mountains and quests and adventures.
I would revisit the slowness of her laying on her back in the hills
behind her house,
Blanket spread over rocks
And goat heads,
Cows grazing just beyond the crest,
Gazing at clouds above, watching them morph and change as we
assigned them characters.

I would revisit the times she spent next to the creek by her
house,
Pant legs wet from crossing blue-green water,
Ankles sore from slipping on algae covered rocks that lived on
the bottom.
She spent those days resting on leaf beds of her creation,
Following barely there new trails,
Watching birds and slowly and meticulously picking up rocks for
the collection,
Pretending they were gems,
And she was a queen.

The best part of her day
Was watching the butterflies dance,
Bright sun on her shoulders, feeling the freckles of a new tan kiss
her collarbones,

Spending hours on the phone with her best friend.
The most stressful part of her day
Was choosing what book to flip through first,
Which fork in the trail to follow first.

I would return to those days because they were easy.
Only animals that were friends too,
Story book characters,
Only blisters on heels
From walking barefoot
On the hot dirt and dusty fields.

There were no parents arguing,
No pressures at work,
No rigid rules,
No male gaze,
No beauty standards,
No masks to put on,

There was just me,
Wild and free.

WHITE FLAG

Why is so hard to
Just admit that I don't want to be here

Without the sirens
The phone calls
The hospital gown

I wish I could say that
Right now
In this moment,
Covered in
Covered in
I don't know if it's sweat or tears
But it's salty
It burns like a fire that's
Saying please let me go home.

It's not that I want to die but
It's that I don't much feel like
Living
In this moment, In this body
In this time
Quarantined in my own body,
The same hellscape
That I fought so hard to ignore
For the last seven years,
Isolated in the crime scene
Wasteland
Desert swamp
That I call my skin.

I'm not thinking of plunging the
Corkscrew in my neck
Because of how hard I fought to stay breathing.
I'm not going to lose blood after all
The nights of lost sleep,

Every tired morning spent with war paint
Just to fall asleep having lost another battle.
But sometimes

Sometimes I just want to wave the white flag, to surrender,
To rest

BUILD A WOMAN WORKSHOP

I am a customizable build a Bear woman,
Always made of the same stuffing, the same zippers, the same
black bead eyes,
But something always different on the outside.

Is it true that no two snowflakes will ever be the same?
If so, I am a snow storm, greeting everyone with a different
version of myself.

Maybe I'm not a snow storm - maybe I'm pieces of a leftover
birthday cake in the break room,
Every chocolate slice is what makes me whole, but everyone is
welcome to
Pick and choose.
"I just want a small piece," someone says, so I use a knife to serve
the smallest part of myself, careful
To not take up too much room on the plate.
Someone uses a plastic fork to scrape the frosting off the top,
Experiencing only the parts of me they find
Enjoyable.
Half-eaten slices are discarded, abandoned in the trash next to
Old coffee filters and chewed up, flavorless gum.

For once, I want to be the snowflake instead of the storm, the
whole cake instead of the pieces, the book instead of the dog-
eared page, the meal instead of the free bread beforehand, the
person instead of the position, which is to say... all of me is
welcome.

FRIENDSHIP IS...

A warm cup of tea that warms the belly on a winter night, snow
falling, air chilled.

The freedom to choose
The family your soul craves.

A way to love the self deeper.

A hand that is always holding yours,
Even when you don't see
Anyone else on the path.

Surprise texts that say
How are you
And they want to know
Your answer.

Time that passed too quickly.

Silences that don't need to be filled.

The overlapping harmony of giggles that feel breathless
And also
The unstifled rhythm of tears and shoulders touching.

An emergency contact.

A single flower that gently opens to the sun,
To see herself surrounded in a field of wildflowers.

The phone ringing.

The smiling
Hello

Too many cups of coffee
And nibbles taken from pizza crusts.

Trust falls that don't feel like falling.

A heart opening.

NOT EVERYTHING I GIVE YOU IS A PRESENT

When I speak, my words are a confession,
My *I love you*'s are apologies,
Every action is me bartering for your opinion of me.
When I ask how you are doing, what I really need to know is "do
you like me?"
I can be anything to anyone -
Can be anyone to everyone.
I call myself flexible,
"I can get along with everyone!"
But what I really mean is,
I need to get along with everyone.
Every conversation is a case study, beginning like an exam,
Ending with me wondering if I passed.
What I really mean to say, is,
It ends with me knowing that I failed.
Every day starts the same:
Putting on the masks, drinking the coffee that keeps me bubbly,
wearing the dress that makes me approachable, never looking at
my eyes in the mirror.
It always ends alone, just me in my body,
Sore from twisting itself to meet the expectations of who I ought
to me,
Racing thoughts of ever encounter stuck in my tired mind.

I want to end poems with a neat bow,
Like I do with my sentences,
Trying to find a way to
Downplay what I've said, to say
I know I just said a lot,
But don't worry,
I'm fine.

But maybe I'm not fine, and maybe
I don't have a bow to offer you,
Maybe just being tired
Just being anxious
Just being lost
Is enough for you right now.

PERSEPHONE'S DAUGHTER

When I remember my rape,
I no longer see the rapist, with his
Shaggy blonde hair and
Pot stained breath.
I no longer see the van with its drawings,
With its sleeping bag on top of the
Mattress in the back.
I see it like the crow saw it,
Leaves falling everywhere, the young girl
That is me
Leaving herself.
I see a young goddess,
Defeated from war, naked,
Front side torn open,
Persephone's daughter with her insides
Turned out, bleeding on the
Wild field of grains and crop.
I see the girl
That is me
Dead,
Giving what's left of herself to
The wild animals that gather
For a feast, to devour what's left of her.
I see her eyes close,
The switchblade next to her face
My face
Paint that was applied to impress
Streaking the raw, red cheeks.
My cheeks.

I no longer want to kill the man who hit me,

85

No longer want to slash the Volkswagen tires,
No longer want to see his flesh bleed open to the vultures like
mine did.
I feel sad for him, though no
Tears will never fall on my harvest for him.
I pity the boy who stripped that girl,
Who has to live with his reflection
Who has to wake up every day with
My blood under his fingernails.
The horror he must feel to remember
The screams and the two lettered word
That drifted up past the van, past the crow, and seared into his
memory.

When the leaves fall from the trees,
Colors like pumpkin pies and apple cider,
Or like fiery flames coming to earth,
Only to land underneath your feet,
I don't see myself burn.
The leaves no longer represent the death
That happened to me by the river.
The leaves are my mask, the parts of myself I can shed,
That no longer can grow as part of me.

TO THE GIRLS

You will be taught that your voice
Is white noise,
That your thoughts are just dreams,
That your dreams are just fantasies;
Unrealistic.
You will be taught that your opinions
Are just irrelevant,
That your needs are just suggestions,
That your suggestions are just words;
Meaningless.
You will be taught that happiness
Is fleeting,
That your joy is just a feeling,
That your feelings are just emotions;
Unimportant.
You will be taught that your body
Is sinful,
That your desires are just prayers,
That your prayers are just cries;
Unanswered.

You will be taught
To quiet your voice,
To be seen, not heard,
To be grateful for what you do have,
And to never ask for anything else.
You will be taught
To love,
To understand,
To fear,
To shrink.

You will be taught
To shame
And to be shamed.

To the Girls,
I want to teach you
To be loud,
To shatter dishes
To sing birdsongs in the park
To kick dirt between your toes
I want you to be known.
To fight
For the life you want,
To enter the ring when you've been wronged,
For your knuckles to form small blisters,
Reminder of your winning battle.
I want you to know
That you deserve love,
That you deserve an abundance of love without having to work
so hard for it,
You deserve warm coffee brought to you in bed
To taste soft cupcakes with frosting without guilt,
To have someone bathe the parts of your back you can't reach,
Then later brush out your knots before kissing you goodnight.
You deserve sweet dreams.
I want unconditional love
To be a phrase that you can comprehend.
I want you to look in the mirror,
And embrace yourself with the grace of wearing your Sunday
dress
Or your mom's lipstick gently applied like a whisper,
That grace you so often give to others.
I want to teach you not to fear anyone or yourself.

To not be afraid of shadows,
To sleep with windows open,
To ride that bike down the hill by your friend's house,
Hair down and your hands off the brakes.
I want to teach you to accept, not to hate.
I want to teach you that your tears are brave,
That being sensitive is not an insult.

To the Girls,

I love you.
I want to teach you to love yourselves, too.

Printed in the USA
CPSIA information can be obtained
at www.ICGtesting.com
LVHW040805060923
757193LV00006B/138